In Went Goldilocks

Out went **Papa Bear**.
Out went Mama Bear.
Out went Baby Bear.

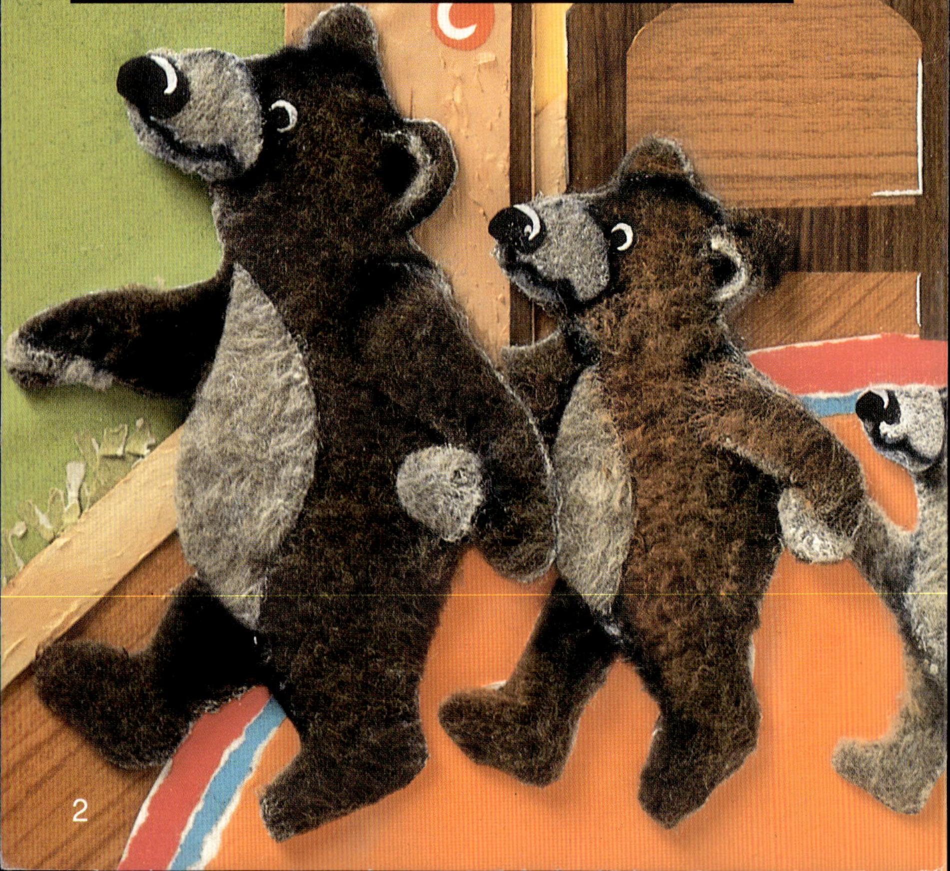

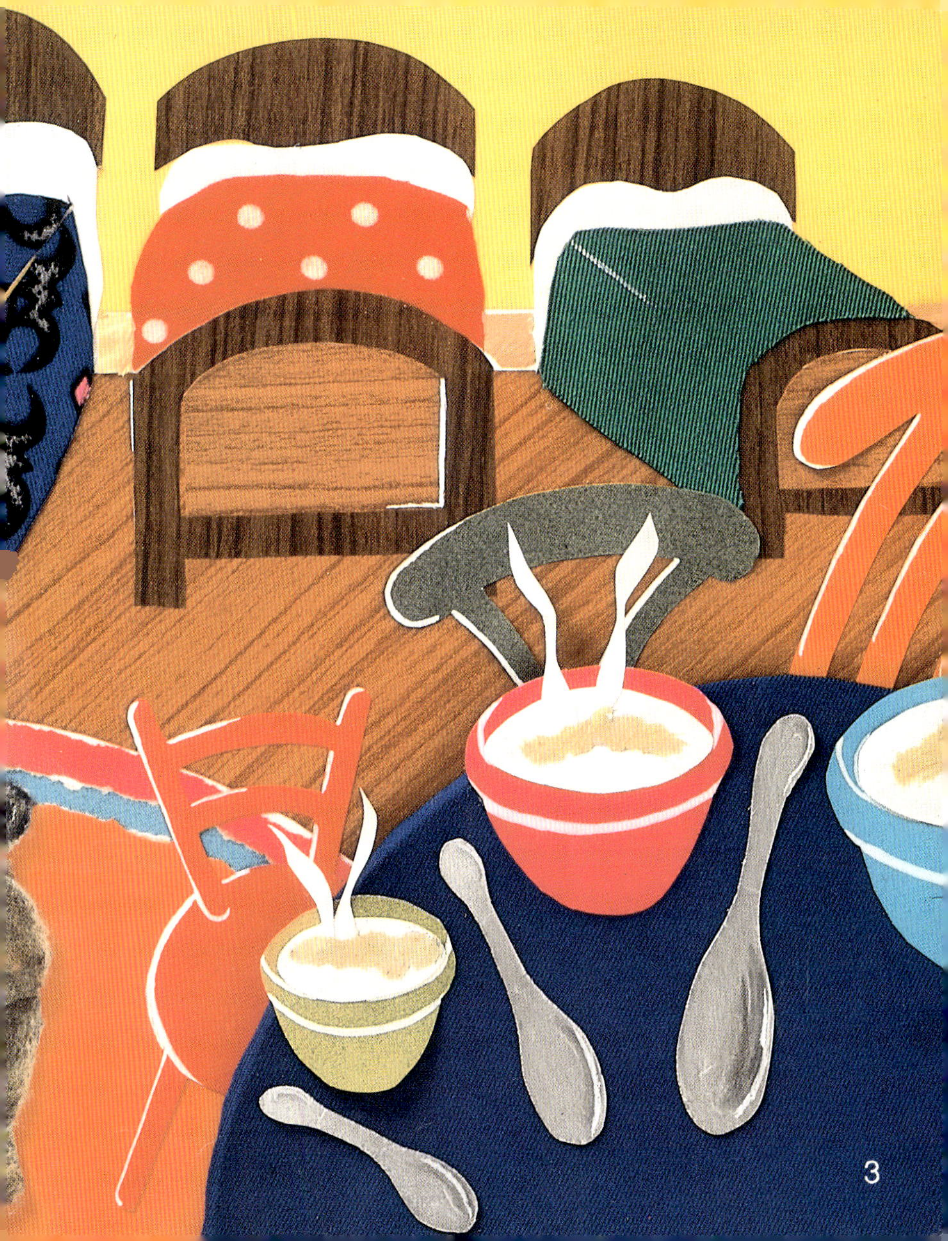

In went Goldilocks!

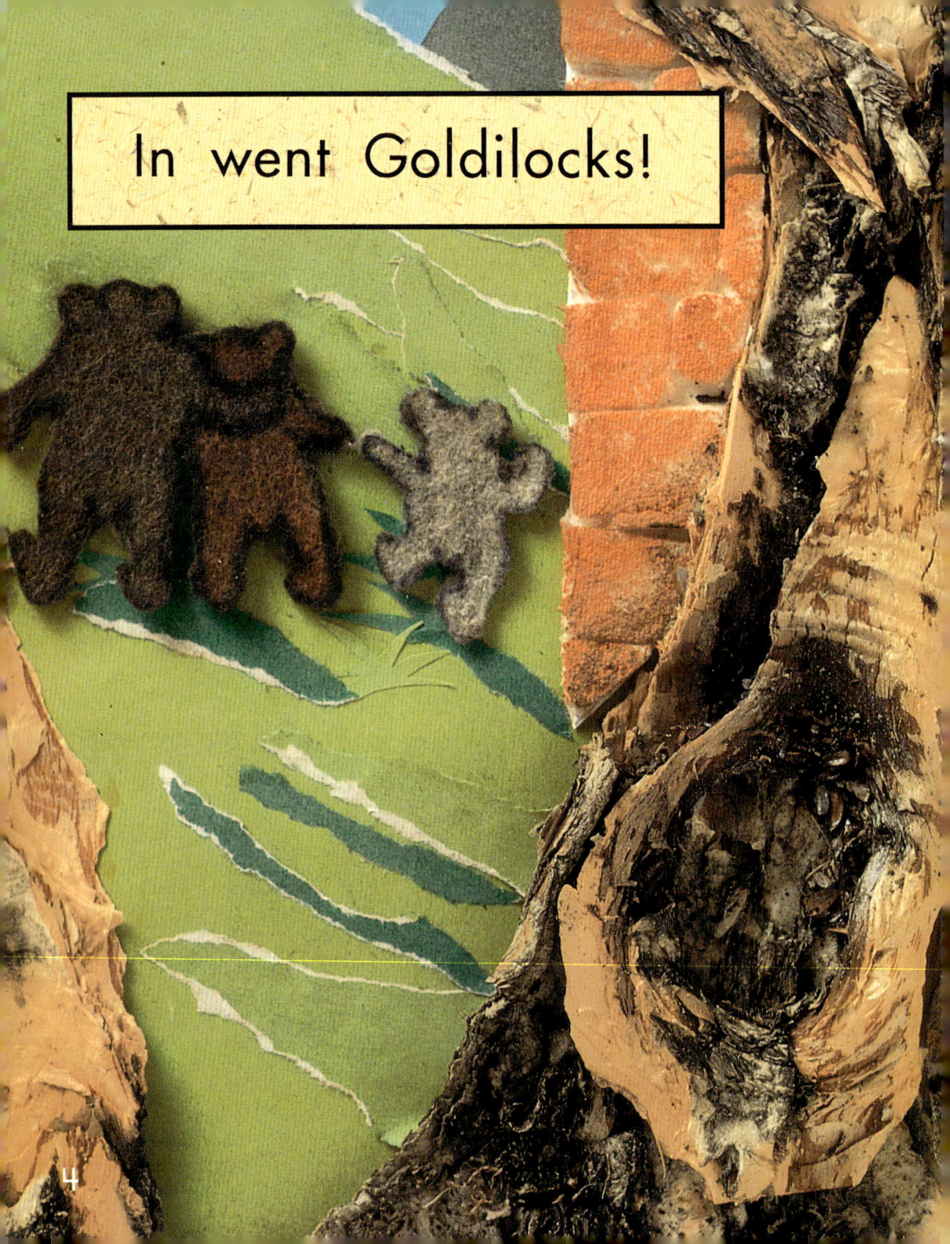

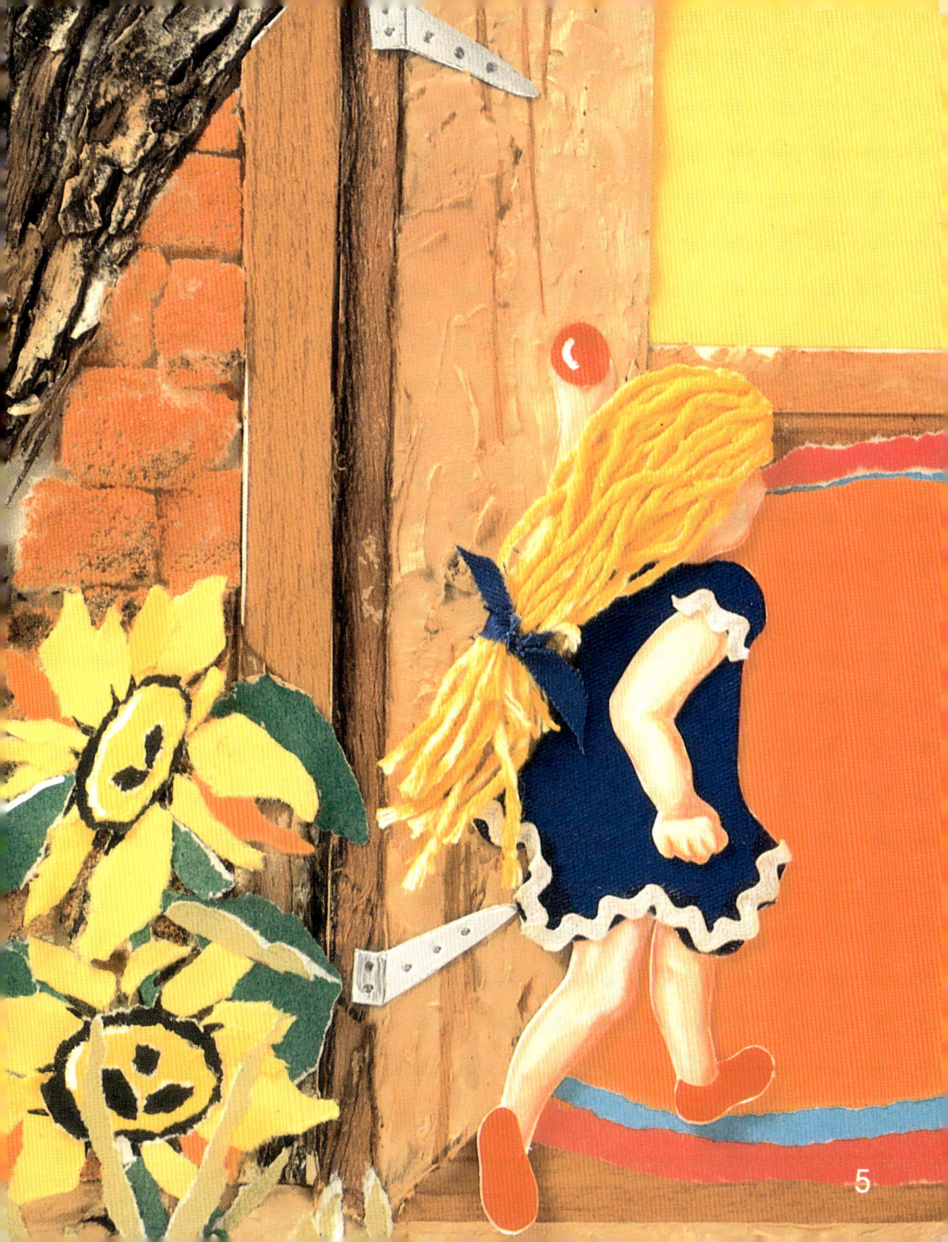

Back came Baby Bear.
Back came Mama Bear.
Back came **Papa Bear**.

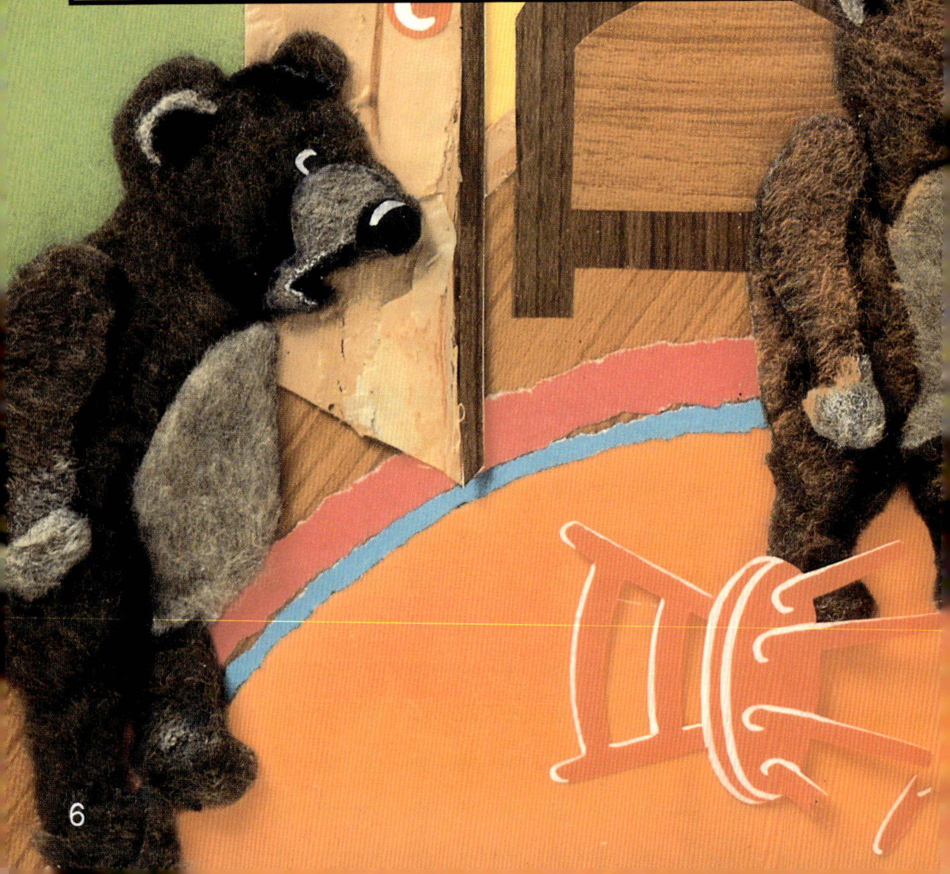

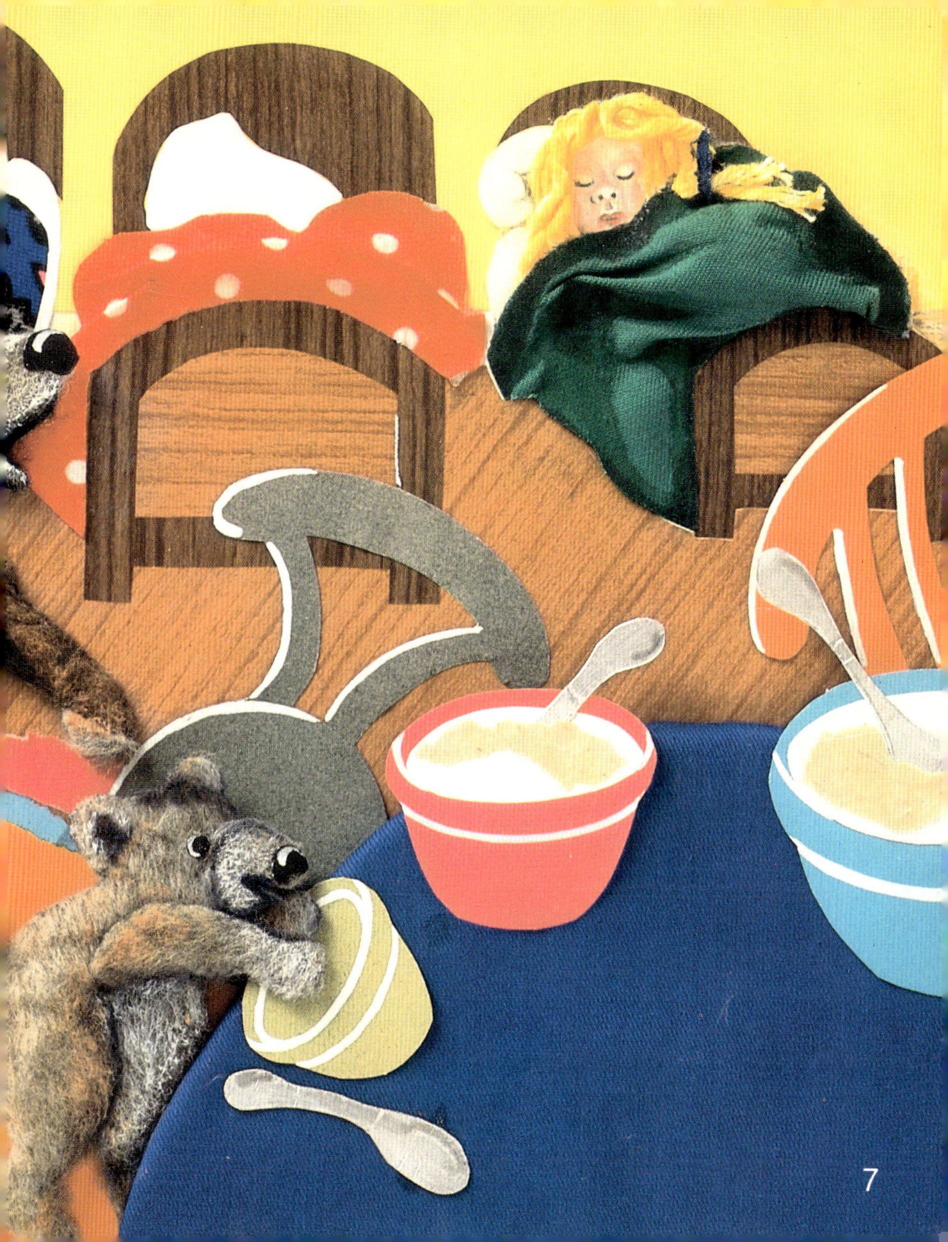

Out went Goldilocks!

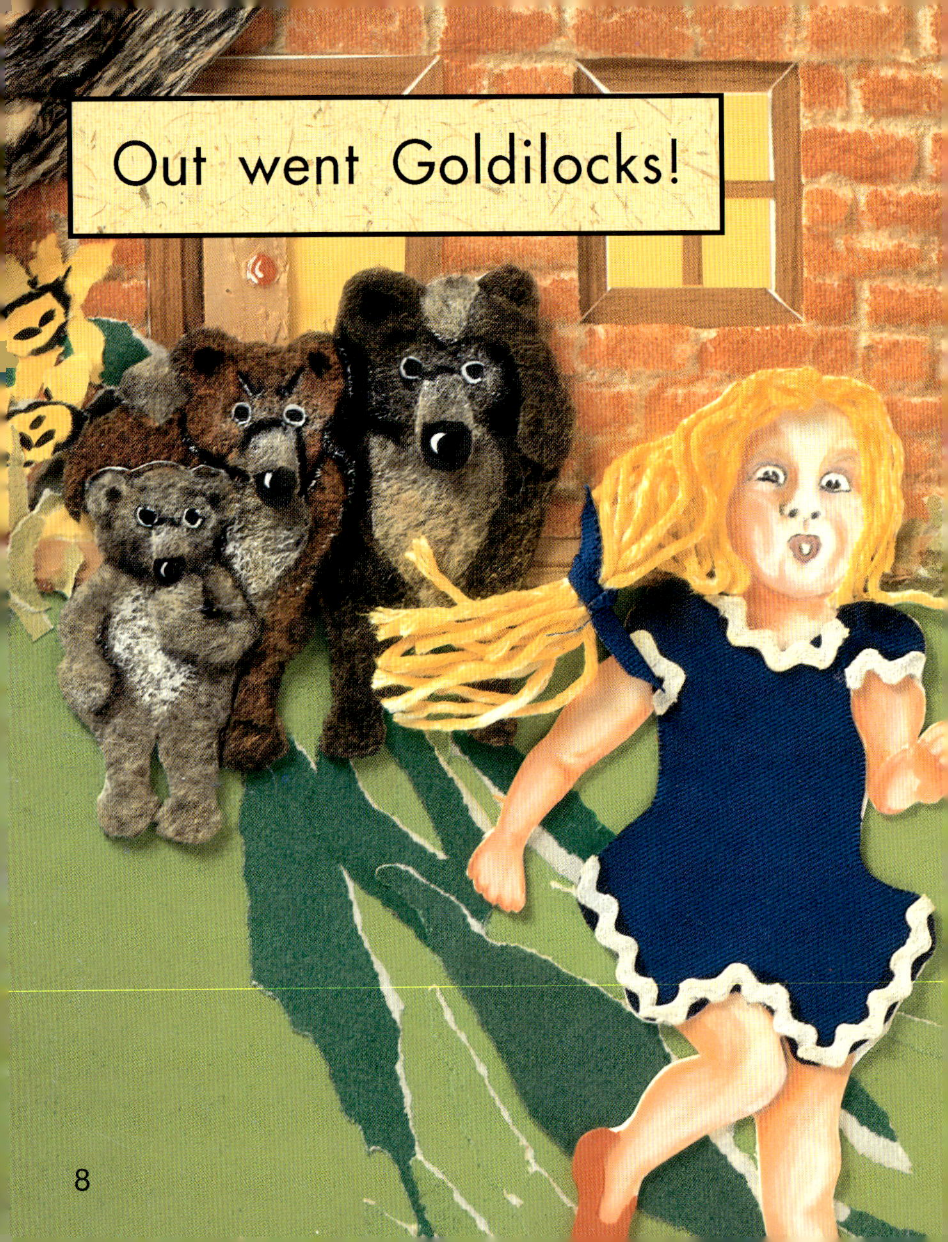